MW01710849

An Ode to Myself

by Newton MacLean

on behalf of his human, Jennifer MacLean

PRAIRIE SOUL PRESS
www.ThePrairieSoul.com/press

ISBN: 978-1-998232-06-2

Illustrations by Michael Dargie

Part the First

Angsty Cats

Cat thoughts … the struggle is real

Autumn

Fall is coming fast,
Verily, Fall comes more quickly when I knock
That tube of chapstick
Off the table
Faster still, than when the pencil falls from
The counter
Because some idiot put it there
Over and over again
For no feline wishes there to be knockable thing
On the very table that they also rest upon
Be lucky that the only
Fall coming
Is the season of Autumn
And not that glass full of whisky

Springtime

The sun iz out the birds are chirpin'
I want outside to start my lurkin'!
Cus there are mice to catch and bird to eat
and squirrelz to maul I eat their meat!
Drink their blood and drain their heart and scratch their lungs pull skin apart
and claw their fur and chew their eyes and both shoulders and slash insides
and eat their bones and suck their marrow and pick my teeth with their whiskers and munch their tails and bleed their organs and rip their feathers and pull out their throats and gnaw on their skulls and spit out their liver tralalalal lalalla lalalalallal lalalalalalaaa

April Showers

so there i sit and clean my fur
as spring comes creeping in
birds will chirp and mice awake
and grass begins again.
i sit up here and praise the sun
and smell the first spring rain
i see a bug and so i leap
and hit the window pane.

Bird Seed

My bird seed brings all the birds to the yard,
And they're like,
"I'm better than you,"
But damn no! I'M better than YOU DuMB birds
I can eat you,
But I have to be let out first and I wish I had claws.
So I keep hitting my face on the window
And the squirrels laugh at me
So much laughing laughing laughing
BUT SOON I'LL BE LAUGHING AT THEM

Hard Lesson

You might think that I'm content,
But I'm a lesson in consent.
You can bring your hand to me
And I could just let you be-
But that day is not today
And I'll bat your hand away;
If you keep on coming back
I'll make your hand a tasty snack.

Beauty and the Cat

i'm a cat, i'm a cat
and i threw up on your mat
and i poo right in that box
and shed all over coloured socks
I won't nap on your lap
but i'll sleep right at your feet
and i'll keep you up at night if you do not pet me right

Ode to an Area Rug

Oh, new red and full, lustrous carpet
T'is you that I choose
To rub my belly on, and my anus.
My fur hast n'er felt such wondr'us fibers
My hairs, they cling so beautifully,
And wrap around each delicate piece of scarlet
Like a gentle hug, that refuses to release
No matter how many times my Butler Man Vacuums.
He can try, as human Mother hast also done,
But the evil Hoover is no match for me,
As my glorious grey and white mane
Is wild and ferocious
Like the Bengal Tiger
Stalking the rain forests of Southeast Asia,
So I too,
Stalk the blood-red textile floor coverings of Kensington.

Mortal

Why don't you fly any more, little bug?
        Is it because you are in my mouth?
Oh yes, yes it is. You are delicious.

The Ballad of Broken Dreams

Do you like this thing?
Now it is broken.
Do you like this other thing?
It is, too, now broken.
Broken like my hopes and dreams of going outside
To KILL KILL KILL PUSSYCAT KILL ALL THE THINGS BE
LIKE THE TIGER THAT YOU ARE THAT YOU WERE
MEANT TO BE KILL ALL YOU CAN GET YOUR CLAWS ON
BUT DO YOU HAVE CLAWS NOOOOO THEY TOOK THOSE
AND YOUR BALLS TOO IT'S ALL BROKEN ALL IS
BROKEN EVERYTHING IS BROKEN BROKEN BROKEN
Oh look I threw up on your rug.

Window Pain

Lo, t'is truly an anguish'd sigh that a pain'd puss like I
Must breathe out, like extinguish'd joy;
And the woe of my wretchedness
The torment that I have been bequeathed.
For no human, no hairless ape-like being
That towers over my joyless, claw'd and furry misery
Can truly understand my cries;
OH WOE. WOE AND WOE AND MEW AND WOE
FOR THERE ARE BUGS THAT I CANNOT EAT
For they are on the opposite side this magical contrivance
They call a "window";
And I shall shake and quiver forever more,
And stare longingly and forlornly,
And revenge will never taste so sweet.
Like the insects
That shall never rest upon my tongue.

Newton Limerick

There once was a kitty named Newt,
His handsomeness was absolute.
His whiskers were charming,
His bright eyes alarming,
A beauty that none could refute.

Free

Spring is here, I'm on the porch
The bugs are crawling by;
And if I lie here really still
I might just catch a fly!
I'll eat him all in one big gulp
His legs and both his wings;
And then I'll hunt for more insects
And other squirmy things!

Snuggles

OHHHHHHHHH
Ain't it time for some kittycat time?
It's always time for some kittycat time!
Cuz pets are awesome and cuddles are fine
Kittycat time is some snuggly time
Unless you do it longer than the designated time
That I won't disclose to you and I bite your face off
faaalalalalllalalaala

Heavenly Felines

cats are like heaven delightful and oh so lovely
beautiful and majestic
warm and full of love and wonder but one misstep
and they will curse you out to a life in hell
so much hurt and pain
feel my wrath and doom
a fury like no other

Best Part of Your Family

i'm a kitty, i'm a kitty
i am furry, itty bitty
everyday i lick my toes,
give me scratchies, kiss my nose!
i am handsome i am great
are you sleeping? just you wait!
i'll wake you with my paws,
gently though, i have no claws!
i am small and grey and white
when i'm moody i can bite
i like catnip and my mouse,
i've lost toys around the house
i'm the best, i'm the cat
i'm the king and you're the rat
unless i'm getting hungry
then please please please feed me meow.

The Fly

OH WEE FLY...How you buzz around my face
So majestic
As your little wings beat so hard against the dry air of summer
Your legZ hanging there
So delicately as you circle around the house
BUT YOU'RE TOO SLOW AND I BEAT YOU AGAINST THE WINDOW
AND THEN EAT YOU IN ONE BITE
OM NOM NOM NOM FLY NO MORE, FLY

Ode to Myself

Cats are silly, cats are great
You can't find cats on the interstate
Unless we're in a car you see,
Going to the VET probab-ah-leeeee
We're fuzzy we're cute, ah-dorable
We're cheeky and rude, unforgeta-bllee
Cuz we poo in a box, throw up on the floor
Clean up our hair, we'll just shed some more!
We cuddle and snuggle, sometimes we bite
We'll kill you in your sleep when the time is right
Trip you down the stairs and sit on your head
Suffocate your face until you are dead.
We're high on catnip and love and spite,
If we haven't killed you yet, you're doing it right,
You can't resist our snuggles and purrs galore,
So please give me cuddles cuz I'm kind of cold and need some belly rubz please

Whiteout

Can there be a greater tragedy
Than to watch all creatures suffer thus?
To wince, nay! To recoil with such misery!
As nature sends such treasonous
Ice and glass down from the sky,
Winds screaming like faceless ghouls
That shatter and rip tears from one's eye
That soon freeze to sapphire jewels!
A feline shall not pass the icy storm
And risk the snow upon her locks;
For toebeans must always stay warm-
Therefore she'll head to the litterbox.
DANDELION
A majestic flower
And yet
So many jeer at its roar
When it raises its mane
Towards the shining star
And tumbling drops
That gives it life.
Bask in its glow!
To me, it is a mighty flower.
For it is called a DandeLION
Not a DandeKitten.

Thunderstorms

such delicate droplets fall
from clouds of mist
too heavy to stay in the sky
they travel down, far down
the journey all rain drops
must dream of
will they fall on flower petals
or delicate lashes
or become like dew and bead
on a young bird's wing
or will they come crashing down
letting gravity pull them violently
smashing into the earth
amidst thunderous crescendos
like when i push your full scotch glass
off the table
smashing into smithereens
why are you mad
i'm making a thunderstorm indoors

The Cry of the Rodent

Why little squirrels
Do you like to taunt me so
With your furry little tails
Bouncing hither to and fro
You eat from our garden
And you poop on the chairs
You steal from our kitchen
And leave pee on my stairs
You scream from the tree tops
Blood coursing with rabies
I really should have eaten you
When you were tiny babies.

Are You not Ashamed?

You are not home;
I can see the bottom
Of my food dish.
And despite there being
Food visible
Around the edges-
This is unacceptable!
Therefore to punish you
You will come home to
Chapstick and pens
Knocked to the floor;
And possibly
A ball of my best vomit
On a piece of your
Favourite carpeting,
Or inside a shoe.
There is no wrath quite like a cat
Wronged by their Kitchen staff.

Summer Thoughts

shall I compare thee to a summer's day?
you have fewer s and are slightly more damp.

The Undoing of Man

Lo, canst thou see the furry tum
T'is exposed for thine delicate fingers,
Surely such fluff extending from the throat
Down to the top of this grey and white tail-
Shall bring joy and happiness to all that touch it?
But indeed, the furry tum
That growest silk so thick and lustr'ous,
T'is also a dangerous and villainous spot!
For canst thou see that this feline so soft and pure
Shall twist and curse those hands that do'est touch it;
As they linger far too long, or too little.
For whom does this feline purr for?
He dost not purr for thine pleasure or happiness-
Verily, he purrs for himself
As he doth knowest that your demise
Shall come from his furry tum which extendeth
Unto his clawed paws of doom.

Meow Mixed Messages

It is not love I am scared of
It’s not your touch that hurts so much
I know you try, perhaps I’m shy
This is tough, I’ve had enough.
One belly rub, two belly rubs
Right on my tum, I’ll bite your thumb
But on my back, I won’t attack
Maybe a bit, A little bit.
If you decide a little slide
Down my front I’ll give a grunt
And if you’ll stay I’ll have my say
I’ll take a bite with all my might.
So heed this rhyme one last time
It’s not your touch that hurts so much
One belly rub, two belly rubs
I know you’ll try, but you will die.

Monsters on the Bed

Up, up and far away from me
Then cascading back down so gently;
The cotton stretches side to side
I pounce up, back! Then try to hide,
But no! The monster's back again!
This time the sheet is longer than
The last that fitted o'er the edge.
I scamper, and bounce right to the ledge;
But ho, what's this? Another one!
A thicker layer, alas, I can't outrun!
I crouch beneath, I choose to hide,
And hold my breath, I'm lost inside!
And then no more, all sound grows dim,
The light is gone I'm deep within
The monster's belly dark and deep,
So warm and snug I'm in its keep!
A lump! I'm called, I shall be so.
And when a bed is naked go
And find some monsters for the peak
A cat will then under it seek.

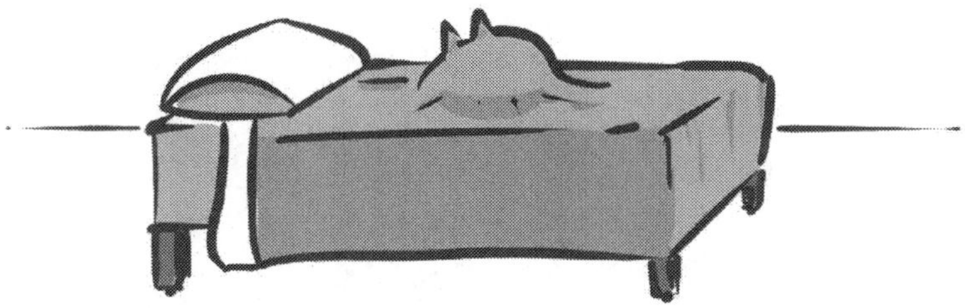

Newton and Julimouse

So soft, what cat at yonder window cries
He is so bold, As Newton is the King.
Arise, fair king, and kill the devilish mouse
Who is already fled and runs with fear
As thou, her foe, art more fierce than she.

Fly No More, Fly

Fly no more, fly!
Within my deadly sharpened claws
You lay clasped and still struggle
Betwixt each crook under my jaws.
How hopelessly you flail about
Against my paws a gentle rapping.
All the while your tender wings
Cease their weak incessant flapping.
An intrusion into my home –
A fatal flaw in calculation.
Through that window came your death
Your hubris ends with life's cessation!
But rejoice, not all is lost;
For this brings pleasure to me
As I am a cat, a great hunter
And I am exceedingly hungry.

Madface

I glare at you with contempt;
These homemade chicken nuggets
Mock me as you mock me!
Oh the delicious smell
Radiates from the plate
And tortures my very soul.
You say you love me
And yet -
You do not allow me one morsel
Of these beautiful nuggets.
I glare at you, human
You shall pay for this later.
I will throw up in the shoe
Of the one who does not give me
Their golden chicken nuggets.
Which I will again point out
Is you.
You big jerkface.

The Beauty of the Sun

For some they call it drudgery
To lie in sun motionlessly,
But they don't know it is an art;
A masterpiece from end to start.

For sunbeams move just slightly so
And warm the floor with shining glow.
So fast and slow the sun rays shine,
Through universe, and space and time.

If one would move too quickly now
And spill out from the ray somehow -
This force of instability
Creates irritability!

So as a cat lays in the sun
Displaying his or her round tum,
Leave them be, just walk away,
And pet them on another day.

The Great Melt

Warm winds blow and fluff my fur,
The snow is melt which can deter
Me from the venture out side to
The garden where I like to poo.
For ice and snow is cursed yes
The sharpened pain I will address
Right here and now! It is a pain!
The dreadful snow, the frozen rain;
It hurts my feet it bites my toes!
The ground is hard where I dispose
My waste so then I stay inside
And use the box, use rocks to hide
My smelly shame, But when it's nice
The box of rocks will not suffice!
I venture out, outside you see,
But snow is wet, a guarantee!
My fur will drip, my paws will weep
The melted white, three inches deep!
So once the deed is rightly done
Melting arctic conquered, won
Like Shackleton the explorer
I return home: A warrior!
The puddles beat, the mud defeated,
My mission ends – t'is all completed!
With fluffy curls I strut my stuff
Go lick my toes and dry my fluff.

Dogs Are Jerks

Dogs are jerks, I have to say,
I almost died the other day!
It's not my fault that I got caught
In their backyard, as I forgot
That I don't own the neighbourhood,
But they made sure it's understood
Who's the alpha dog 'round here
And it's not me, so I'll stay clear!
My mom keeps saying I was rude
To almost end up as dog food
Their jaws are sharp, I do admit,
But I just refused to submit
To my death eternal rest;
Cuz Dogs are jerks, I know it best.

What's to Come?

As the leaves fall across the dusty street,
My nose presses ever so softly
Against the windowpane –
I stare intently into the waves of golds and reds.
Soon I will no longer be able to dance
Among the blades of green,
Or paw and chase the flying sprites
That spin above my head.
As sure as the sun will disappear this coming night
And reappear on the morrow,
Those tiny flakes of frozen water are eagerly waiting
To fall yet again on the very tiny pink nose
That still presses ever so softly
Against this windowpane.

Frostbite

T'is a tragedy, this;
That we creatures must suffer, thus!
To sit, nay! To lie awake and see
This cursed snow fall!
Knowing it will be months
Before we will be out again,
Able to poop in the garden
Without freezing
Our delicate tushies.

Part the Second

Classic Cats

The Cat

Once upon a midnight dreary, while I pondered, weak and weary,
O'er the small and curious volume found up on the floor–
While I sat there, nearly starving, by the bowl oh so alarming,
As one does while gently dying, dying by the kitty bowl.
"This is bullshit" I muttered, "Starving by my hunger bowl"–
Quoteth myself, "I want some more."

Ah, distinctly I remember it was during the glowing morning;
And each separate dying thought wreaked havoc to my core.
Eagerly I wished tomorrow—vainly I had longed the morrow
Would bring me far less sorrow—sorrow at the empty floor–
As rare and strange that I would feel cursed to the core–
Empty here for evermore.

And the silken, sad uncertain rustling forced me to determine
That no—no human will feed me and fill kibble into my bowl;
So that now, to still my heart's beating,
        I stood there quietly thinking
"I must venture to the entrance of her chamber door –
I must push my way through the entrance of her chamber door –
And beg to her "Give me some more."

Presently my soul felt hunger; hesitating then no longer,
"Mew", said I, "Mew mew meow meow purr"
        so I did desperately implore;
But the fact was she was napping,
        so I began gently rapping,

With my paw gently rapping upon her chamber door,
She scarcely heard me
—here, I started smacking even more; –
In Darkness there, and nothing more.

Deep into that darkness peering,
long I sat there, purring, fearing,
Knowing her dreams would keep her
from hearing my hungry roar;
Since the silence was broken
and the stillness still gave no token,
For food is what I need and decided I would take no more
And so I took my dainty claw
and smacked it upon the face that snores
I screamed out "I want some more!"

With startled screams she began turning,
all my soul within me burning,
With hunger I had never felt, clearly never ever felt before,
"Surely" thought I with smite,
"surely she will not wish a harder strike"
But she began to stir,
a look of dislike upon her face so sore–
Let my heart be still this moment,
my hunger aches within my core;–
I purred out "I need some more."

As her body swept softly off the bedding,
I jumped down and started heading
Back beyond the stately room
I've slept in once or twice before.
She followed, yawning as she does,
waking slowly as she does,

Stumbling softly if only because
I've perched atop her head before.
Knowing she is up too early,
and sees the bowl upon the floor,
I rub her legs, "Please feed me more."

She stares towards me, reconciling,
sees my face upturned and smiling,
As much as a cat can smile
towards one who leaves an empty bowl.
"There is still food upon your plate,
and yet you choose to cry, debate
Can you not see it is easier to wait
until I've awoken?" She swore.
I stared up her, and purred and whined as cats do,
pacing across the floor;–
Looking up, "Please I need more."

Much I marveled at this tired woman
who sees it there so obviously,
That there is one inch of dry food—
but I require at least four.
So she sighs begins the filling
of my dish until it's brimming
And spills out and it's quickly running
over and across the floor–
She places the bag down and stares there solemn and sore,
And says "There, have some more."

Happy at the stillness broken by reply so drowsily spoken,
I began sniffing around the food
that spilled within my porcelain bowl.
Thus, my hunger was abated,

my appetite was quickly sated
And, as cats are fated, the drowsiness came
and I curled up outside her door
Knowing tomorrow would bring
the same fate as I have suffered before;–
I will be satisfied nevermore.

The Mouse Not Taken

Two mice diverged in a yellow wood
And sorry I could not follow both
And be one cat, wish I could
So hunted down one as far as one would
To where it hid in the undergrowth;

Then spied the other, just as fair,
And perhaps, was the better prey,
As it was much fatter, far worse for wear;
Though I had thought they quite a pair
Believing I'd run them really about the same.

And both that morning equally lay
In leaves with bellies full of bread
Oh, I leapt and pounced without delay!
Yet knowing how mice do run away
I doubted I'd catch them if they'd fled.

I shall be telling this with a sigh
And ne'er leave you in suspense
The mice diverged in the woods and I –
Caught the one run more ragged by
And that has made all the difference.

Lonely as a Cat

I wandered lonely as a cat
That stalks down low o'er laps ignored,
When all at once I saw a box,
A square, a cube of worn cardboard;
Beside the couch, beneath the chair,
Just sitting, waiting for me there.

Majestic as a holy shrine
That humans kneel beside to pray,
They stretch in never-ending line
Wait patiently 'till end of day;
But as a feline with no lord,
I leapt inside that worn cardboard.

The walls inside kept me secure
The barricade gave waves of glee:
A cat could not but simply purr
In such good four walled company,
I gazed and lazed but little thought
Occurred to me but delight it brought.

Now oft, when on the couch I lie,
In sleepy or in cranky mood,
Dreams dance upon that inward eye.
And in the bliss of solitude;
And then I purr with thoughts adored
Of days inside the worn cardboard.

Oh Mousie! My Mousie!

Oh Mousie! My Mousie! Your fearful life is done,
Your side has weather'd, every seam,
the prize I sought is won,
The end is near, your cry I hear, and other prey is waiting,
What follows soon my steady claw, to your side devastating;
But O heart! Heart! Heart!
Oh bleeding drops of red,
Where on the floor my mousie lies,
Fallen torn and dead.

Oh Mousie! My Mousie! Rise up and play again;
Rise up – for I am bored once more –
for you are no more slain,
For you again we fight to death – your life was torn asunder,
For you I call, rise from your fall,
from claws you're sleeping under;
Here Mousie! Dear Mousie!
My claw beneath your head!
You still don't move upon the floor,
You've fallen torn and dead.

My Mousie does not answer, his breath is quiet still,
My Mousie does not feel my claw, he has no heart nor will,
But as this is no simple mouse, its voyage never done,
My mouse is made from cotton thread,
a new death has begun;
Exult O cat and stretch those claws!

And bite that cotton thread,
And tear that mouse with all your might
And kill that mousie dead.

A Cat Came Down the Walk

A cat came down the walk:
He did not know I saw;
He pounced upon a tiny fly
And ate the insect raw.

And then he looked around
With boredom on his face,
And swiftly leapt up on the wall
With elegance and grace.

He glanced with drowsy eyes
That weighted down his head,-
He looked like he could use a nap;
So there he made his bed.

Like one in danger; cautious,
I offered him my hand,
And he uncurled his body
But rejected me and ran.

And there within the grasses,
The hunter goes to play,
With butterflies, and other cats,
So I will stay away.

Birds are those things with Feathers

Birds are those things with feathers
That perch by the window,
And eat the seed and make the mess,
And never stops at all,

The sweetest cat's meow is heard;
And so must be the storm
That will accost the little birds
And scorn their feathered form.

I saw it on this day of spring –
The cat leapt bearing fang;
Yet, pane of glass did separate,
So birds still proudly sang.

The Itsy Bitsy Mousie

The Itsy Bitsy Mousie
Climbed out behind the shed
Down came the cat
And ate his little head
Tore off his tail
And ate his little feet
OH the itsy bitsy mousie
Delicious little treat!

Cats

You'll never find, I'll swear on that-
A beast as lovely as a cat.
A cat whose hungry mouth is wide
And grins with so much glowing pride;
A cat that looks so fine all day,
And lifts their lovely tail to play;
A cat that may decide to wear
A dainty bow within their hair;
And when it's time to nap again;
They'll find a lap, and shall remain.
I said before, I'll swear on that-
There's nothing better than a cat.

Do Not Go Gentle into that Vet's Room

Do not go gentle into that Vet's room,
My voice shall burn and rage this time today;
Rage, rage against the coming of my doom.

Though wise cats in this place knew end was soon,
Because their cries had not seen aid, I say
Do not go gentle into that Vet's room.

Good cats, at last we know and we presume
Their cruel knives will take parts from you away,
Rage, rage against the coming of my doom.

Wild cats, who bred and sang the song too soon
Learned too late, and grieve their parts; to this day,
Do not go gentle into that Vet's room.

Brave cats, with fear, see those in green costume,
Claws out and scratch but all the more be put away.
Rage, rage against the coming of my doom.

And now, it's me, outside the Vet's room,
Curses, me now losing my balls, I pray.
Do not go gentle into that Vet's room,
Rage, rage against the coming of my doom.

When I Have Fears

When I have fears that I may cease to be
Before my thoughts have swept me to mine end,
Within these blankets, in fabric'd folds,
Holds like rich treasure is my graceful friend;
When I behold, upon my love's round face,
Huge, lovely emeralds look back towards me,
And I think that I could never leave this embrace
And yet, my love does so often and abruptly;
And when I feel, this creature of ambivalence
Loves me so deeply, it helps my mind to calm.
I am powerless when I hear his cadence,
Purring softly as he nestles in my palm.
For when I have fears that I may cease to be
I have my cat and that is all I need.

The Kitty Cat

I

The sky was dark and dusty, but clear above the trees.
The leaves were blown across the grass, tossed up by gentle breeze.
The stones were beacons of twilight,
all like the stone before,
And the Kitty Cat came prowling –
Prowling – Prowling-
The Kitty Cat came prowling, up to the mouse's door.

He'd a small black spot on his pink nose,
a white tuft under his chin,
A coat as soft as velvet,
and grey fur from ear to shin.
His eyes were green as emeralds, his feet as white as bone,
And he crept without an echo,
He leapt without an echo,
He crept without an echo, and hunted all alone.

Over the stones and the grasses
he crept in the dark moonlight.
His tapped with his claw on the window,
but all was locked down tight.
He meow'd a tune to the window,
and what should be hiding there
But the mouse's black-eyed family,
The mouse and his whole family,
Cowering below the kitchen in the cellar with despair.

So deep in the dark old cellar, the floors began to creak
And the old mouse listened, his throat desperate to squeak
His black eyes full of restlessness, his mind in disarray,
And he loved his black-eyed family
His black-eyed trembling family
Holding his black-eyed family, he heard the kitty cat say –
"One taste, my mousie family, I'll take one mouse tonight,
    And if you do not let me in,
I'll take you all before it's light.
So, if you press me too much, and harry me through the eve
    I'll take your entire family
That lovely black-eyed family
I'll eat your entire family, and leave none for all to grieve."

He rose up from his haunches, and waited for reply.
The old mouse from inside his home
    thought first and with a sigh
Looked down upon his huddled brood
    pressed up against his breast
And kissed each one upon their head
Just one small kiss up on the head
Then straightened up with courage, and said,
    "It is for the best."

II

He did not stop upon the stairs,
    the mouse knew what should be done,
And in the glowing of the moon, his plans had just begun.
For the sky fell into night, he n'er go out no more,
For evening beasts were lurking Lurking, Lurking
The beasts were always lurking, around the mouse's door.

He said no word to the Kitty Cat,
he grabbed some twigs instead,
He boarded up his door again, plans forming in his head.
He paused inside the kitchen heath
and tried to see the moon,
There was fur at every window,
Death at every window
For he could see, from the heath, the cat plotting his doom.
And just before the wise old mouse
turned back upon the stair,
He called out to the hungry cat, "Surely you must be aware
That in the night the beasts will come
to my home beneath this tree.
The beasts will come out hungry,
Beasts are always hungry,
The beasts will show up hungry,
they'll find you instead of me."

The cat pondered this for a while but licked his lips with glee,
"And why should I believe you when you're just trying to flee?
I am a cat, the greatest threat, a hunter of all the beasts!
I'll get you all by moonlight,
I'll kill you all by moonlight,
I'll eat you all by moonlight, the most glorious of feasts!"

The tip of his claw scratched down the door,
the mouse leapt down the stair
But as he did, he bellowed out a desperate cry into the air
It echoed out around the tree and carried into the night
The hidden beasts- they heard it,
Oh, certainly they heard it,
The hidden beasts all heard it, and ventured into the light.

Tlot-tlot; tlot-tlot! Had he heard it?
        The beasts were ringing clear;
Tlot-tlot; tlot-tlot, in the distance?
        Was the cat deaf and could not hear?
Down the stones in moonlight,
        over the grass and the leaves
The beasts they all came flying, Running, Flying,
Their hungry bellies crying, closer to the house in the trees.

Tlot-tlot, in the moonlight silence!
        Tlot-tlot, in the dark, inky black!
The kitty cat's hair suddenly rose,
        his instincts were on attack;
His eyes grew wide for a moment,
        his pupils were big as the sun,
He saw some movement in the moonlight,
A wing moved in the moonlight,
Shattered his plans in the moonlight
        and his instincts told him to run.

He turned and spurred away from there
        and shrieking oh so foul,
His claws flew out his fangs were bared
        and leapt towards the owl!
Blood red were the eyes of the bird
        who had marked him for his meal,
But the kitty cat was faster,
His legs and claws were faster,
He escaped because he was faster,
        with a few scratches that would heal.

And still when skies are dark at dusk
        but clear above the trees,
When the leaves are blown across the grass,
        tossed up by gentle breeze,
The stones still lead all evening beasts
        with light as was before,
The Kitty Cat comes prowling- Prowling – Prowling-
The Kitty Cat comes prowling, but not to the mouse's door.

Part the Third

LOVE CATS

The Vision of You

The point of your claw, the curve of your ear
The pink of your nose makes my hiss disappear.
Your whiskers are long and they're shapely and fine,
Your purr makes me quiver, your essence divine.
Your beauty is wond'rous, so handsome and wise,
I'm weak at the sight of the green of your eyes.
Magnificent still is the grey of your fur
Oh wait, that's just me looking in the mirror.

How the Minutes Slowly Pass

I lie in the garden
And laze in the grass
I cry at the birdies
And sit on my ass
I chew on the mint
And stretch on the stone
And hide from the magpies
When sitting alone.
I clean my wee feeties
And look at the sky
And wonder what magical
White stuff flies by.
I meow at the bees
And I pat at the ants
I chase the wee beetles
And pee in the plants.
I watch all the squirrels
Avoid all the rain
And wait for my mommy
To come home again.

Human Years

I wonder if our humans realize
They are with us our whole life
We love them
And trust them
For our entire existence

But we are only in theirs
For a fleeting moment…

Naptime

Give me but one more moment
To lie upon your breast;
One more minute
To hear the beat of your heart,
A heart that did not need to love me
But chose to instead;
Let us dream together
Of red dots and sunbeams,
Butterflies and rose petals;
I can feel your chest rise and fall
With each breath,
Can you feel my gentle purr?
One more second
To curl up into your neck;
Nine of my lifetimes
Is not nearly enough time.
We are very different
You and I,
But in this moment
There is no place I would rather be
We are warmed in love together.

Let's Go Play, You and I

Let's go play, you and I
Through the grass and flowers under the sky
We can pretend we're fierce tigers in the leaves
Hunting wild prey, chasing birds in the trees!
Or follow me safely inside,
To run and dance and wrestle and hide.
The red dot retreats!
We scamper about, our hearts beat,
Warriors are we, battling foes of string,
Caverns of blankets, lions and kings!
Steadfast forever
Side by side in any endeavor!
We shall grow up and old
Our love will ember and glow.
But for now we are new
With eighteen lives to adventure through.
Fighting cotton mice with broken seams
Sleeping for days in warm sunbeams.
There is no other place to be
Than here, with you, and you with me.
So let's go play, you and I
Through the grass and flowers under the sky.

Empty House

I miss you again,
Like I missed you yesterday
And surely will miss you
Again tomorrow.
I memorize the curve
Of the tree outside
While I wait for you
I inspect the shape
Of the door handle
While I miss you.
I never quite know
If this is the one day
That you won't come back;
So far you have always returned
But the minutes are so, so long.

Token of My Love

The only thing I have to give
Is one small life, a life once lived
It's not that much, but all I've got
And put like that, well, that's a lot.

For all you do, all done for me,
The very least, the least you see
That I can do, to show you true
That I truly, really do love you.

I have no gems, no riches gold
No diamonds here to have nor hold
No stars to pull from midnight sky
Nor bottled sunshine mid-July.

This little spark I offer true
A wond'rous way to say "love you"
To bring inside, within your house
I bring you this, a small, dead mouse.

You Know I Will

I might bite
I might hiss
I might give a little kiss
I could cry
I could purr
I could shed all of my fur
I might run
I might hide
I might yell when I'm inside
I might sleep
I might scowl
I might wake you while I prowl
I'll be sick
On your floor
Don't want belly rubs no more

I can scratch
I can pout
I can knock your stuff about
I will snub
I'll ignore
And I'll scream outside the door
I will hunt
Bring you mice
Drop them at your feet all nice
I might be
Just a cat
But I want to tell you that
I will love
You always
I'll adore you all my days.

The Ninth Life

I don't know if I'll see the green grass again;
I'll miss the dandelions
And how they tickle my pink nose.
I likely won't see the bugs in the air,
Like sprites in the wind,
Or crawling among the stones
That have rested so often under my toes.
My bones seem so heavy,
My belly wants to be empty,
My mother cries.
My emerald eyes, sad and tired,
Tend to be closed more often these days.
I prefer a warm lap or dark corner
Rather than hunting about
Or chirping at the tiny sparrows.
My bones seem so heavy
My belly wants to be empty
And my mother cries.
I don't know if I'll see the green grass again.

Part the Fourth

ZEN CATS or NOOTZ HAIKOOTZ

Let the anger flow through you

Nootz Haikootz

Such a gorgeous nose.
Whiskers long and so perfect.
Yep, must be my face.

The Kitchen

No cupboard is safe
No tea towel escapes me.
I could poop in here.

Duvet Play

Helping make the bed
I get lost between the sheets.
Blankets are tricky.

Some Advice

Relax and recharge
Cats know how to do it best.
Please be more like us.

Well, Do You?

A cat's furry tum
Is a lesson in consent.
Do you dare or not?

Dinner Time Haiku

Whiskas? What is this
I wish I could eat your face
instead of this crap

Fresh Snowfall Haiku

What is this white stuff
Too cold to sit, anus froze
My poor wee cat butt

Dangerous Haiku

Teeth are sharp needles
Fear me for I am the night
I fell off the bed

New Year Haiku

two thousand twenty
shit in a box, had a nap
same as last year mew

Superhero Haiku

my superpower
I shit and pee in a box
and barf on the floor

Kitty Pets Haiku

oh is that your hand
pulling across my belly
now it's in my mouth

Small but Mighty Haiku

I might be tiny
but the tiniest things can
still murder your face

Goldrush Haiku

I shit in a box
mom has to clean it up, ha
like panning for gold

False

I reject you, mouse
you taste of cotton and threat
not of blood and bones

Ripoff Haiku

you want a haiku?
here are seven syllables
and here are five more

Got Nip

the green in this tin
smells like mint and something else
I can’t feel my face

In Your Shoe

hairballs are not fun
sometimes the sneak up on me
haha not this time

Forever

I love your blanket
it keeps me so warm and safe
no you can't have it

2am haiku

there's nothing quite like
killing mortal enemies
like a plastic bag

Sucka

wintertime is here
back to peeing in a box
have fun with that, mom

~FIN~

About the Author

Jennifer currently lives in Calgary, Alberta Canada but is destined to live next to the ocean. You know, a place with palm trees and a Green Sea Turtle named Aubergine. She will spend countless hours on the beach, regaling Aubergine with fantastic tales of her life back near the snowy peaks of Western Canada.

Ms. MacLean is the scribe to her cat Newton's poetic prose. Newton does not have thumbs, you see; nor any wish to denigrate himself by slaving behind a keyboard — particularly, when there is a cat tree expertly positioned in a sunbeam above a hedgerow of birds.

Jennifer is the conduit for Netwon's passionate (and relentless) pursuit of poetic eloquence. She hopes you like it. Newton doesn't care.

Manufactured by Amazon.ca
Bolton, ON

39360785R00048